The Little Yellow Practice Book

starring Mrs. Razzle-Dazzle and Friends

Hello! I'm Tap, the music firefly.
Look for me on each page of your practice book!

This practice book belongs to:

Things to do:

1

2

3

4

5

6

Color a key each day you practice!

| Monday | Tuesday | Wednesday | Thursday | Friday | Saturday | Sunday |

Things to do:

1   4

2   5

3   6

Date: _____

Color a key each day you practice!

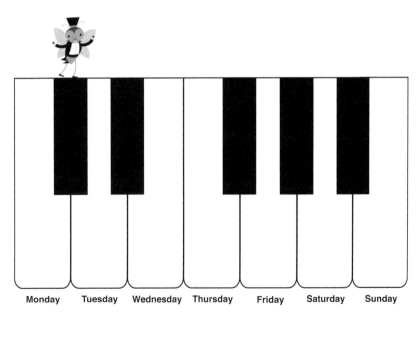

Monday   Tuesday   Wednesday   Thursday   Friday   Saturday   Sunday

3

Things to do:

1

2

3

4

5

6

Date: _____

Color a key each day you practice!

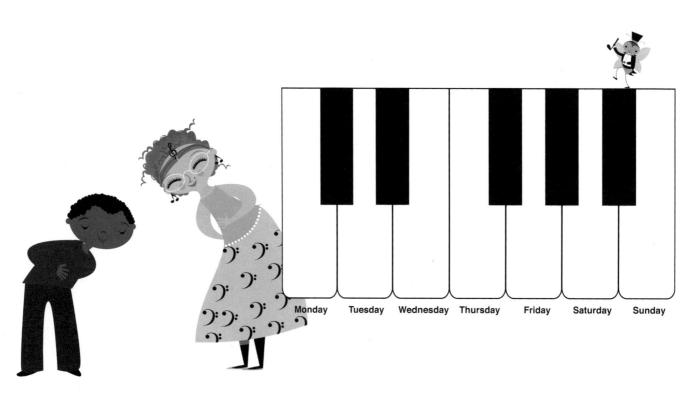

| Monday | Tuesday | Wednesday | Thursday | Friday | Saturday | Sunday |

4

Things to do:

Date: _____

1

2

3

4

5

6

Color a key each day you practice!

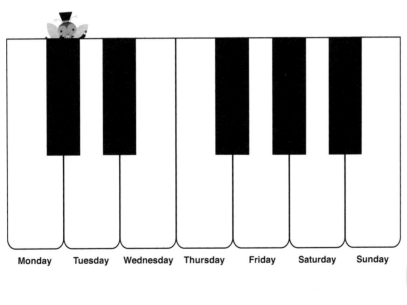

| Monday | Tuesday | Wednesday | Thursday | Friday | Saturday | Sunday |

Things to do:

1

2

3

4

5

6

Date: _____

Color a key each day you practice!

6

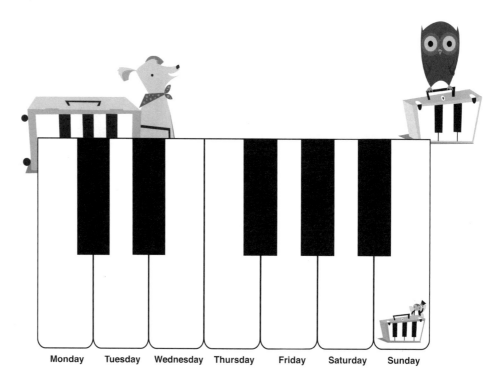

Monday   Tuesday   Wednesday   Thursday   Friday   Saturday   Sunday

Things to do:

1

2

3

4

5

6

Color a key each day you practice!

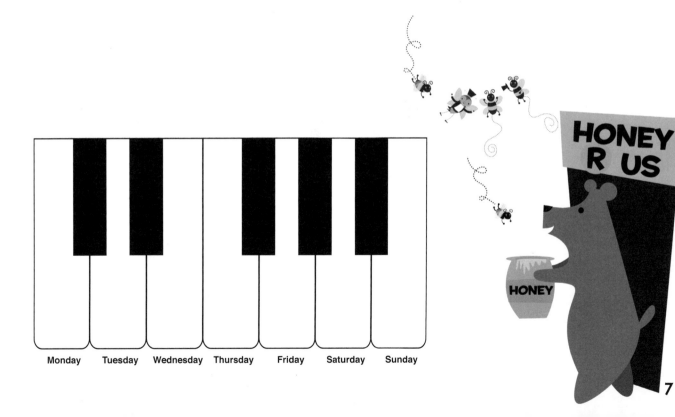

Monday | Tuesday | Wednesday | Thursday | Friday | Saturday | Sunday

HONEY R US

HONEY

7

Things to do: Date: _____

1   4

2   5

3   6

Color a key each day you practice!

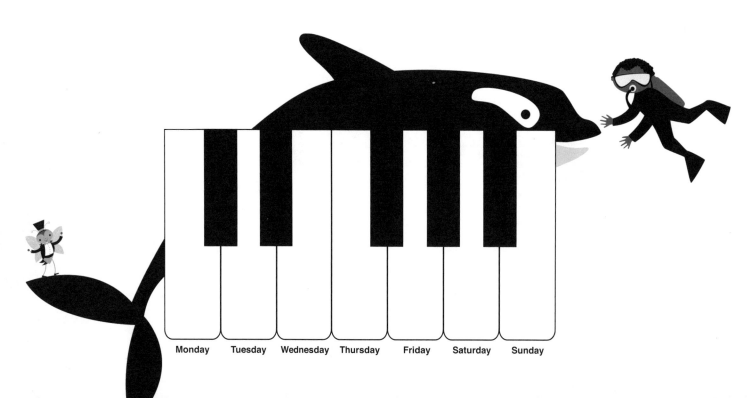

Monday   Tuesday   Wednesday   Thursday   Friday   Saturday   Sunday

Things to do:

1

2

3

4

5

6

Color a key each day you practice!

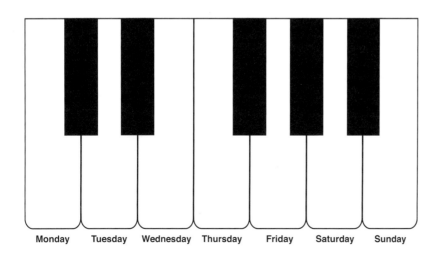

| Monday | Tuesday | Wednesday | Thursday | Friday | Saturday | Sunday |

Things to do:

1

2

3

4

5

6

Date: _____

Color a key each day you practice!

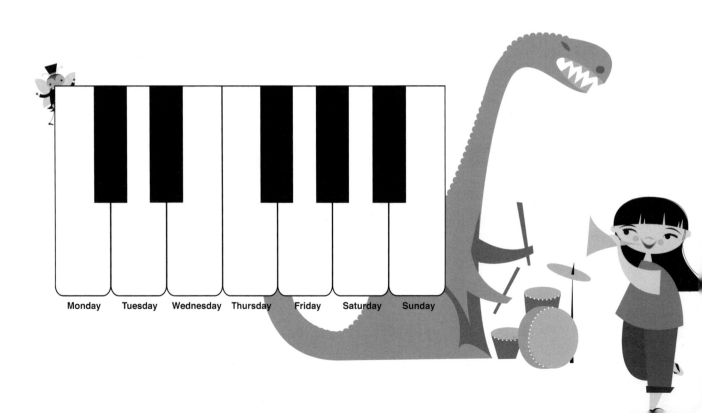

| Monday | Tuesday | Wednesday | Thursday | Friday | Saturday | Sunday |

10

Things to do:

1

2

3

4

5

6

Color a key each day you practice!

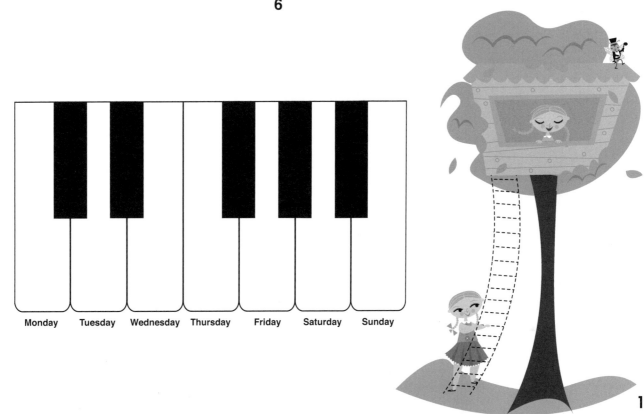

Monday   Tuesday   Wednesday   Thursday   Friday   Saturday   Sunday

Things to do:

Date: _____

1

2

3

4

5

6

Color a key each day you practice!

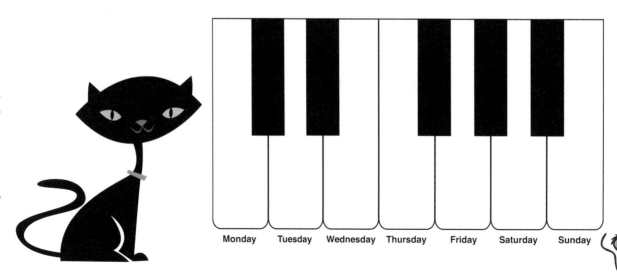

Monday | Tuesday | Wednesday | Thursday | Friday | Saturday | Sunday

Things to do:

1

2

3

Date: _____

4

5

6

Color a key each day you practice!

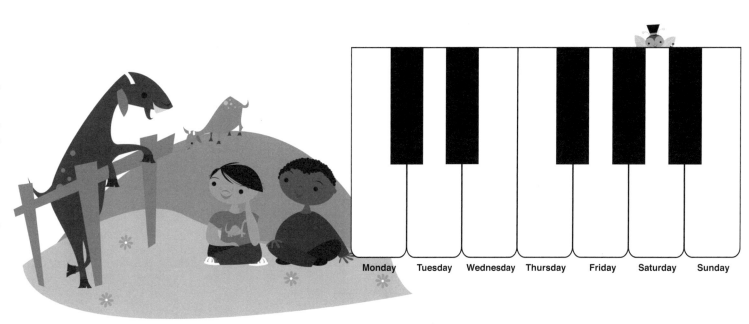

| Monday | Tuesday | Wednesday | Thursday | Friday | Saturday | Sunday |

Things to do: **Date:** _____

1

2

3

4

5

6

Color a key each day you practice!

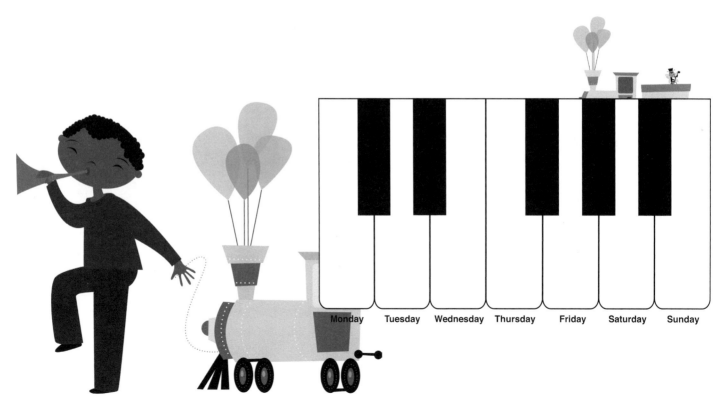

| Monday | Tuesday | Wednesday | Thursday | Friday | Saturday | Sunday |

Things to do:

1

2

3

4

5

6

Color a key each day you practice!

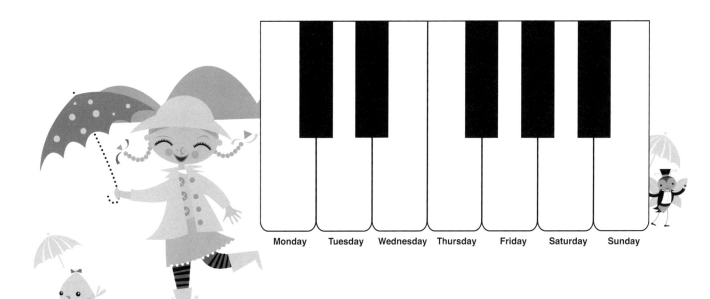

Monday Tuesday Wednesday Thursday Friday Saturday Sunday

15

Things to do:

1

2

3

4

5

6

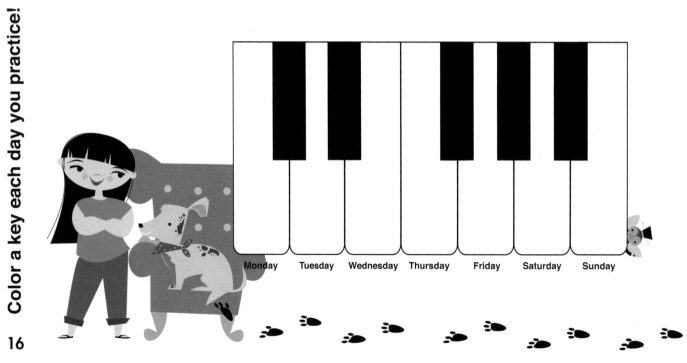

Color a key each day you practice!

Monday Tuesday Wednesday Thursday Friday Saturday Sunday

Things to do:

1   4

2   5

3   6

Color a key each day you practice!

Monday   Tuesday   Wednesday   Thursday   Friday   Saturday   Sunday

Things to do:

Date: _____

1

2

3

4

5

6

Color a key each day you practice!

| Monday | Tuesday | Wednesday | Thursday | Friday | Saturday | Sunday |

Things to do:

Date: _____

1

2

3

4

5

6

Color a key each day you practice!

Monday   Tuesday   Wednesday   Thursday   Friday   Saturday   Sunday

19

Things to do:

1

2

3

4

5

6

Color a key each day you practice!

Monday   Tuesday   Wednesday   Thursday   Friday   Saturday   Sunday

Things to do:

Date: _____

1

2

3

4

5

6

Color a key each day you practice!

Monday | Tuesday | Wednesday | Thursday | Friday | Saturday | Sunday

21

Things to do:

1

2

3

Date: _____

4

5

6

Color a key each day you practice!

22

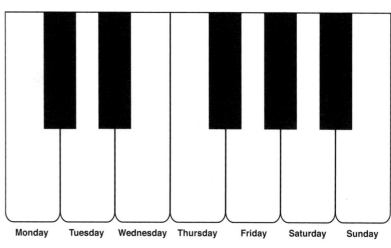

| Monday | Tuesday | Wednesday | Thursday | Friday | Saturday | Sunday |

Things to do:

1

2

3

4

5

6

Color a key each day you practice!

| Monday | Tuesday | Wednesday | Thursday | Friday | Saturday | Sunday |

Things to do:

1

2

3

4

5

6

Date: _____

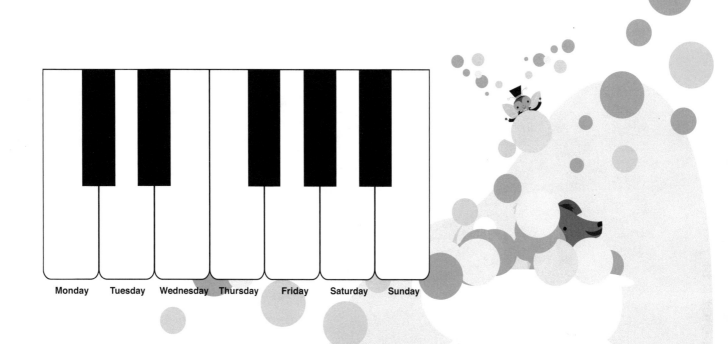

Color a key each day you practice!

| Monday | Tuesday | Wednesday | Thursday | Friday | Saturday | Sunday |

24

Things to do:

1

2

3

4

5

6

Date: _____

Color a key each day you practice!

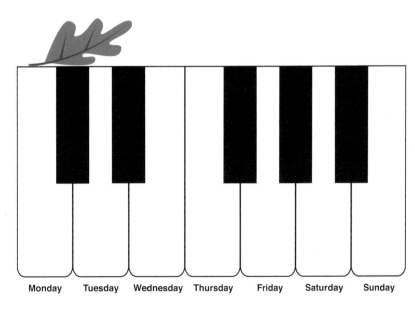

Monday   Tuesday   Wednesday   Thursday   Friday   Saturday   Sunday

25

Things to do:

1

2

3

Date: _____

4

5

6

Color a key each day you practice!

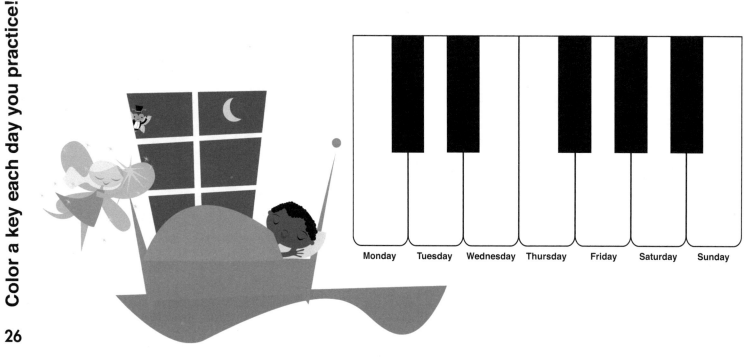

| Monday | Tuesday | Wednesday | Thursday | Friday | Saturday | Sunday |

Things to do:

1

2

3

4

5

6

Color a key each day you practice!

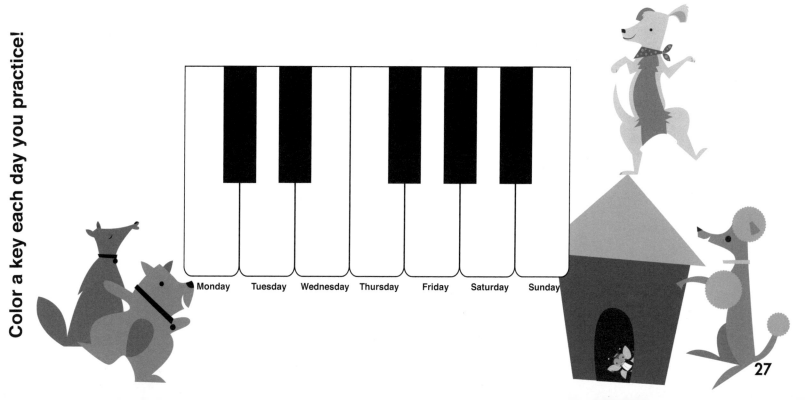

| Monday | Tuesday | Wednesday | Thursday | Friday | Saturday | Sunday |

27

Things to do:

Date: _____

1

2

3

4

5

6

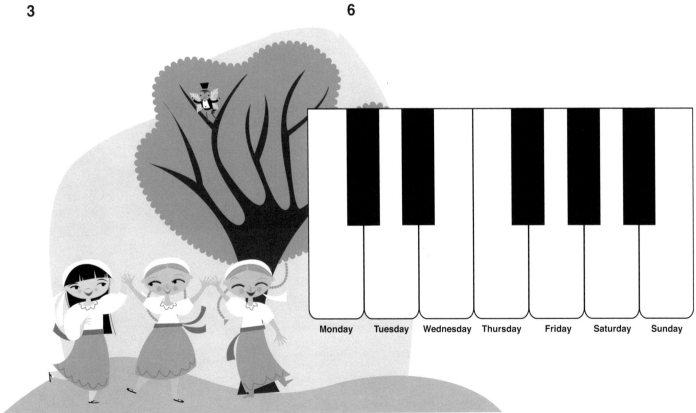

Color a key each day you practice!

28

| Monday | Tuesday | Wednesday | Thursday | Friday | Saturday | Sunday |

Things to do:

1

2

3

4

5

6

Color a key each day you practice!

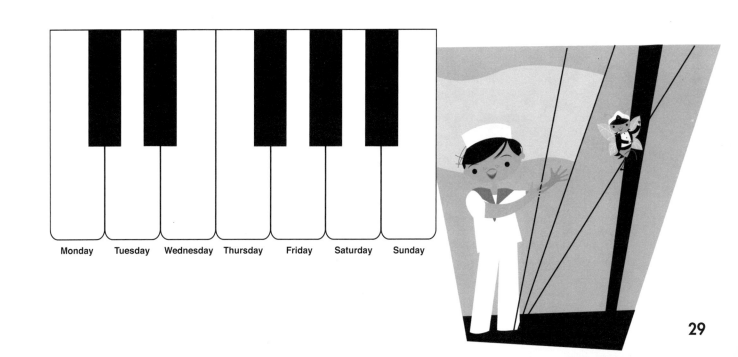

Monday Tuesday Wednesday Thursday Friday Saturday Sunday

Things to do:

1

2

3

4

5

6

Date: _____

Color a key each day you practice!

Monday Tuesday Wednesday Thursday Friday Saturday Sunday

30

Things to do:

1   4

2   5

3   6

Date: _____

Color a key each day you practice!

Monday   Tuesday   Wednesday   Thursday   Friday   Saturday   Sunday

31

Things to do:

1

2

3

4

5

6

Color a key each day you practice!

| Monday | Tuesday | Wednesday | Thursday | Friday | Saturday | Sunday |

Things to do: Date: _____

1   4

2   5

3   6

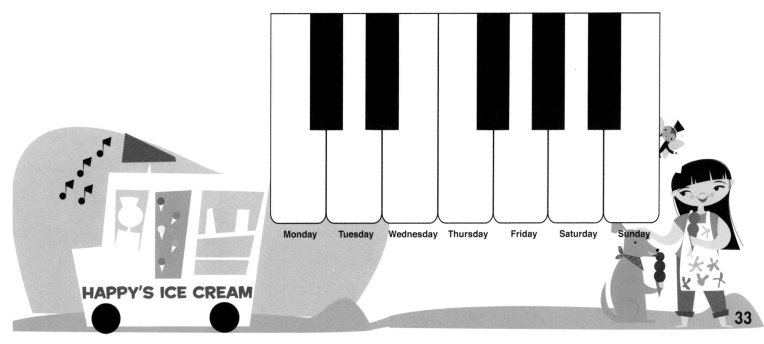

Color a key each day you practice!

Monday   Tuesday   Wednesday   Thursday   Friday   Saturday   Sunday

HAPPY'S ICE CREAM

Things to do:

1   4

2   5

3   6

Date: _____

Color a key each day you practice!

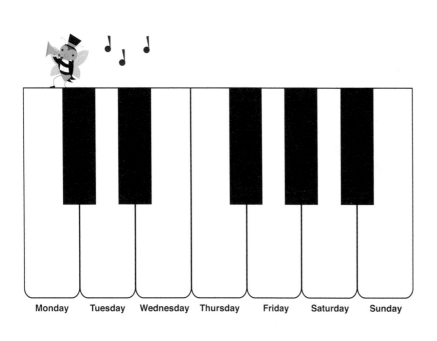

Monday   Tuesday   Wednesday   Thursday   Friday   Saturday   Sunday

34

Things to do:

1

2

3

4

5

6

Color a key each day you practice!

| Monday | Tuesday | Wednesday | Thursday | Friday | Saturday | Sunday |

Things to do:

1

2

3

4

5

6

Color a key each day you practice!

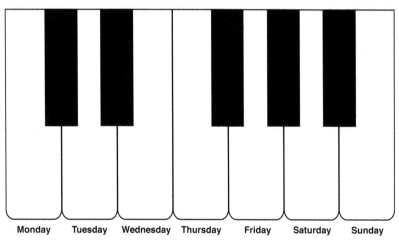

Monday   Tuesday   Wednesday   Thursday   Friday   Saturday   Sunday

36

Things to do:

Date: _____

1

2

3

4

5

6

Color a key each day you practice!

| Monday | Tuesday | Wednesday | Thursday | Friday | Saturday | Sunday |

Things to do:

1

2

3

4

5

6

Color a key each day you practice!

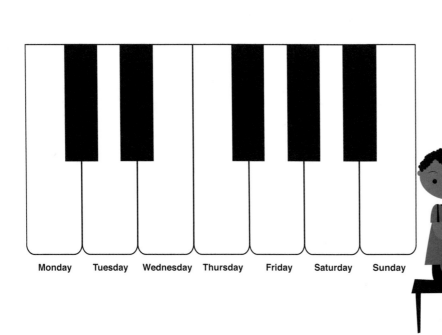

Monday Tuesday Wednesday Thursday Friday Saturday Sunday

38

Things to do:

Date: _____

1   4

2   5

3   6

Color a key each day you practice!

| Monday | Tuesday | Wednesday | Thursday | Friday | Saturday | Sunday |

39

Things to do:

1   4

2   5

3   6

Color a key each day you practice!

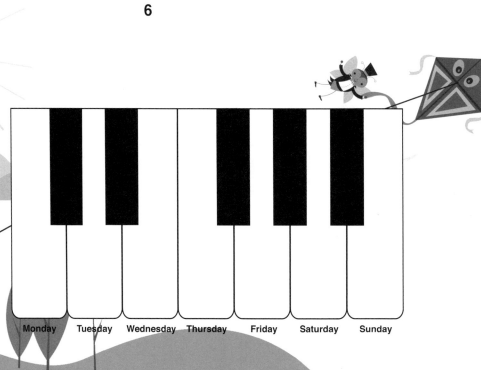

| Monday | Tuesday | Wednesday | Thursday | Friday | Saturday | Sunday |

40

Things to do:

Date: _____

1

2

3

4

5

6

Color a key each day you practice!

| Monday | Tuesday | Wednesday | Thursday | Friday | Saturday | Sunday |

Things to do:

1

2

3

4

5

6

Date: _____

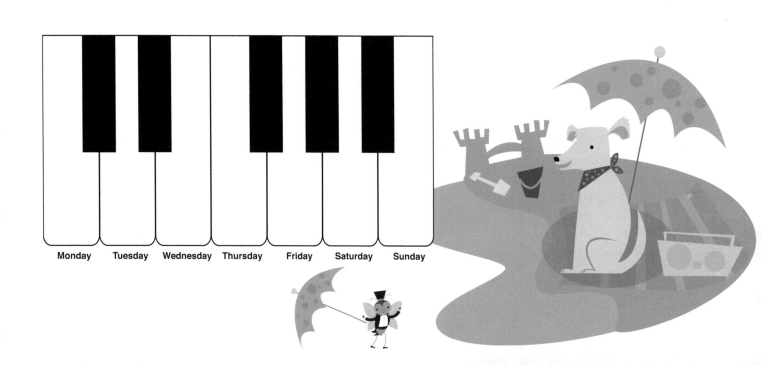

Color a key each day you practice!

| Monday | Tuesday | Wednesday | Thursday | Friday | Saturday | Sunday |

Things to do:

1

2

3

4

5

6

Color a key each day you practice!

| Monday | Tuesday | Wednesday | Thursday | Friday | Saturday | Sunday |

Things to do:

1

2

3

4

5

6

Date: _____

Color a key each day you practice!

| Monday | Tuesday | Wednesday | Thursday | Friday | Saturday | Sunday |

44

Things to do:

Date: _____

1

2

3

4

5

6

Color a key each day you practice!

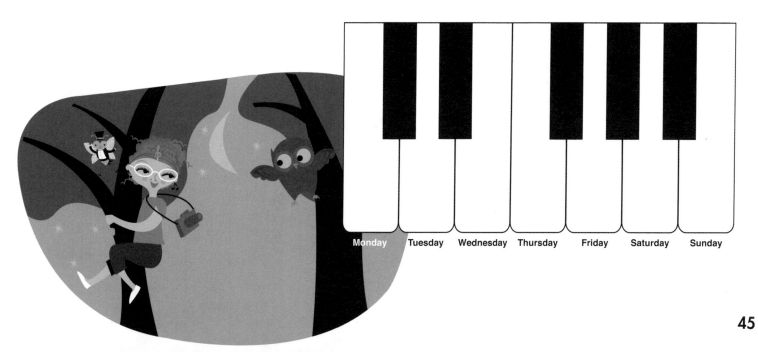

Monday Tuesday Wednesday Thursday Friday Saturday Sunday

Things to do:

1

2

3

4

5

6

Color a key each day you practice!

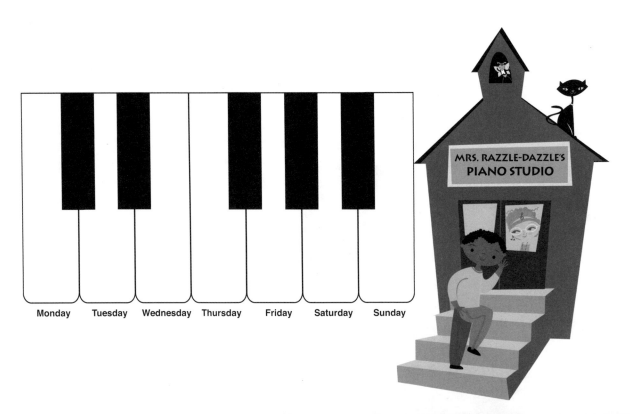

Monday   Tuesday   Wednesday   Thursday   Friday   Saturday   Sunday

MRS. RAZZLE-DAZZLE'S PIANO STUDIO

Things to do:

Date: _____

1

2

3

4

5

6

Color a key each day you practice!

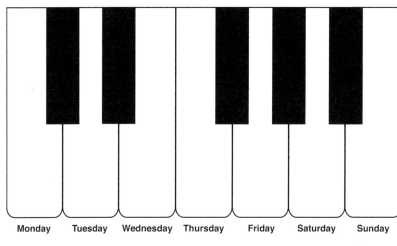

Monday | Tuesday | Wednesday | Thursday | Friday | Saturday | Sunday

47

Things to do:

1

2

3

Date: _____

4

5

6

Color a key each day you practice!

48

| Monday | Tuesday | Wednesday | Thursday | Friday | Saturday | Sunday |